EX Libris

PHILLIP THEVAOS

Letters, Sounds, and Words
A Phonic Dictionary

To Phillip

With love,

Ann Gainey

Christmas 1973

Platt & Munk, Publishers/New York

QUESTOR
A QUESTOR COMPANY

Letters, Sounds, and Words
A Phonic Dictionary

By Linda Hayward • Pictures by Carol Nicklaus

For Bill who thought of the "Eel Page",
and for Eric who wanted to change the labels,
but we didn't.

Contents

j n o

p e

z u v

h g b i

f w t

y c

a r

s l

q x m k

d

When we say words, we make sounds.

We make two sounds to say **at**.

We make three sounds to say **hat**.

Suppose we want to show a word on paper.

We can draw pictures.

We can draw this 🎩 for **hat**,

but how do we draw a picture of **at**?

Suppose we invented pictures for sounds.

It would be a code.

Each picture would stand for a sound.

This picture a

could stand for the first sound in **at**.

This picture t

could stand for the second sound in **at**.

Somebody could look at our pictures,

make the sounds, and say the word.

A long time ago people did this.

They invented pictures for sounds.

The pictures they invented are called letters,

and the letters stand for sounds.

There are only twenty-six letters in the code we use.

We call our code for sounds the alphabet.

There are two kinds of letters:
consonants and vowels.
The difference between consonants and vowels
is something like the difference
between bread and peanut butter.
Bread gives shape to a sandwich
but peanut butter holds the bread together.
Consonants give shape to a word
but vowels hold the consonants together.

Consonants can be anywhere in a word.
When a consonant is at the beginning of a word,
it is called a beginning consonant.
Each beginning consonant in this section
stands for one sound.

BOOM

BANG

BONG

BONK

BOO BA BA BOO

BOING

BING

bells

bagpipes

baton

bucket

bongos

banjo

baritone bird

box BIRD BAND

book

Bird bands aren't bad, but books are better.

p

purple pansies

poodle

parrot

pirate

pelican

puppy

pink porcupine

PEEP PEEP

peacock

people

panda

PARADE

potatoes

pony pulling porpoise

Paraders are peculiar,
particularly parading potatoes.

a yakety yak

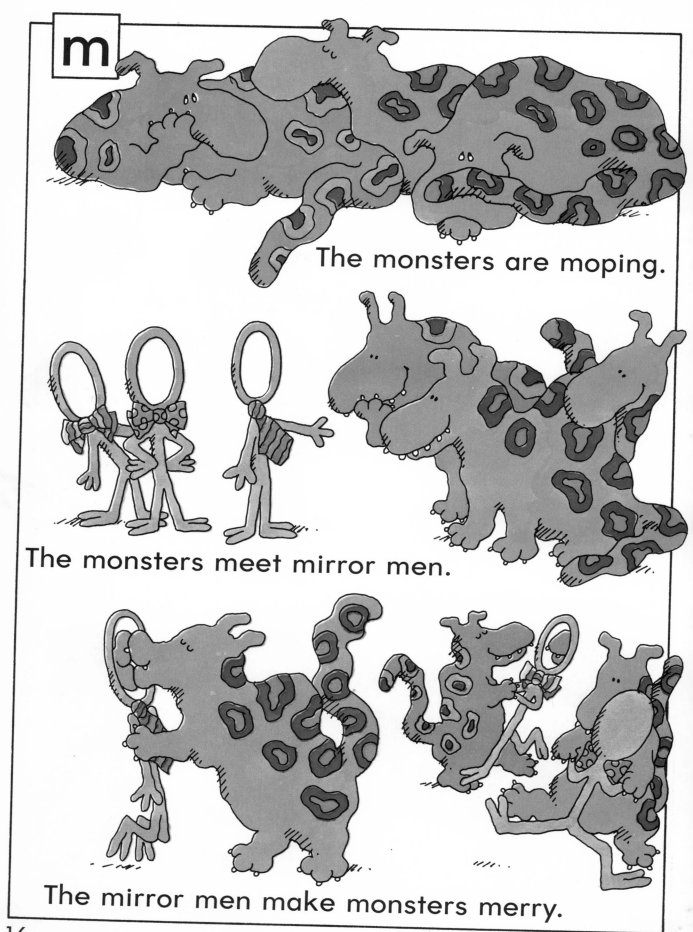

m

The monsters are moping.

The monsters meet mirror men.

The mirror men make monsters merry.

W

wolf waking

wolf washing

wolf weighing

wolf watering

wolf walking to work in woods

18

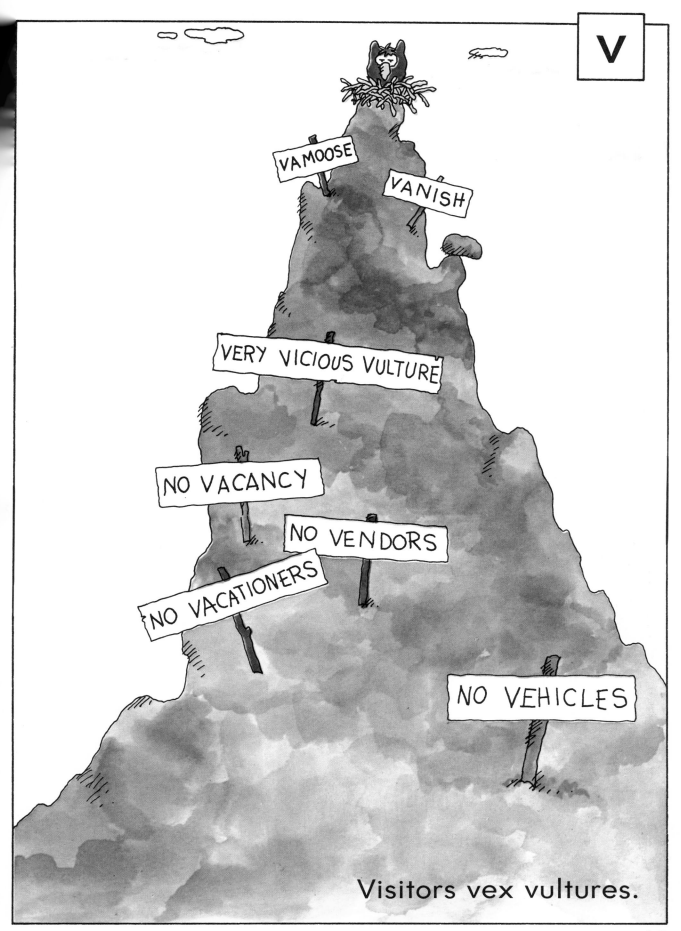

Visitors vex vultures.

The rabbits
in red raincoats
in a row
on a raft
in a race
on the river
in the rain
ran
into a rock.

Rocks are rough on racing rabbits.

hippopotamus with hat

Hello. Hello. Hello.

a hatching in hippo's hat

HOME

at home on hippo's head

A hippo-home has its hazards.

top turtle

turtle tower

ten tiny turtles

Terrific!

TOO TIRED TODAY

TOO TIRED TOMORROW TOO

turtle tucked in tight

turtle taking his time

fat fish

five fish

four foolish fish

I'm no fool.

fast fish

Fast fish feels fine.

Fat fish feels full.

A lizard likes to lurk under the leaves.

A lizard likes to lie low on a log.

Lizards are lazy.

Leaping Lizards! A leaping lizard!

sundae

sandwich

sink of soapsuds

sign seller

sailboat

some seed sacks

six socks

zero zebras in zoo

zigzag zebras

xylophone

bird	jam	people	six
book	jars	pink	so
box	king	pony	some
but	kissing	potatoes	ten
dirt	kite	pulling	time
dog	leaves	puppy	tiny
done	lie	purple	top
door	likes	queen	turtle
down	lizard	questions	visitors
fast	low	quick	walking
fat	make	quiet	washing
feels	meet	rabbits	wolf
fine	men	race	work
fish	needs	rain	xylophone
five	new	ran	yard
four	nice	red	yellow
full	night	river	yes
hat	no	rock	your
head	noise	row	zebras
hello	noon	seed	zero
home	not	sign	zoo

Each beginning consonant in this section
stands for two different sounds.
Usually **c** stands for the same sound
that **k** stands for.
Sometimes **c** stands for the same sound
that **s** stands for.
Usually **g** stands for a sound
no other letter stands for.
Sometimes **g** stands.for the same sound
that **j** stands for.

One reason we have two pictures for one sound
is that people are used to spelling words
in certain ways.

six celeries cycling in a circle on the ceiling

seven celeries with cymbals

celery celebrities celebrating

a genuine gypsy giraffe

cabbages	carrying	cushion	genuine
cages	cases	cycling	gets
camel	ceiling	cymbals	giraffe
can	celery	gang	goat
canaries	circle	garage	gone
canoe	could	garbage	good
car	cuckoo	gasp	gypsy

Some words begin with two consonants.
Some words even begin with three.
Two or three consonants at the beginning of a word
are usually blended.

In a blend, each consonant stands for its own sound,
and the sounds are blended together.
The word **blend** begins with a blend.
The consonants **b** and **l**
come before the vowel **e**.
When you say the word **blend**
you can hear a **b** sound and an **l** sound,
before you hear the **end** of the word.

bl

blurry blob

bluebird blowing blobs

blobs blending

BLOOP

blotched blob

black blob

Blockhead!

Blob-blowers can blunder.

cl

CLUNK
CLONK

CLINK

CLUCK

closet

cleaning up clutter

Cluck?

CLUCK

CLATTER

clumsy clucker climbing on clocks

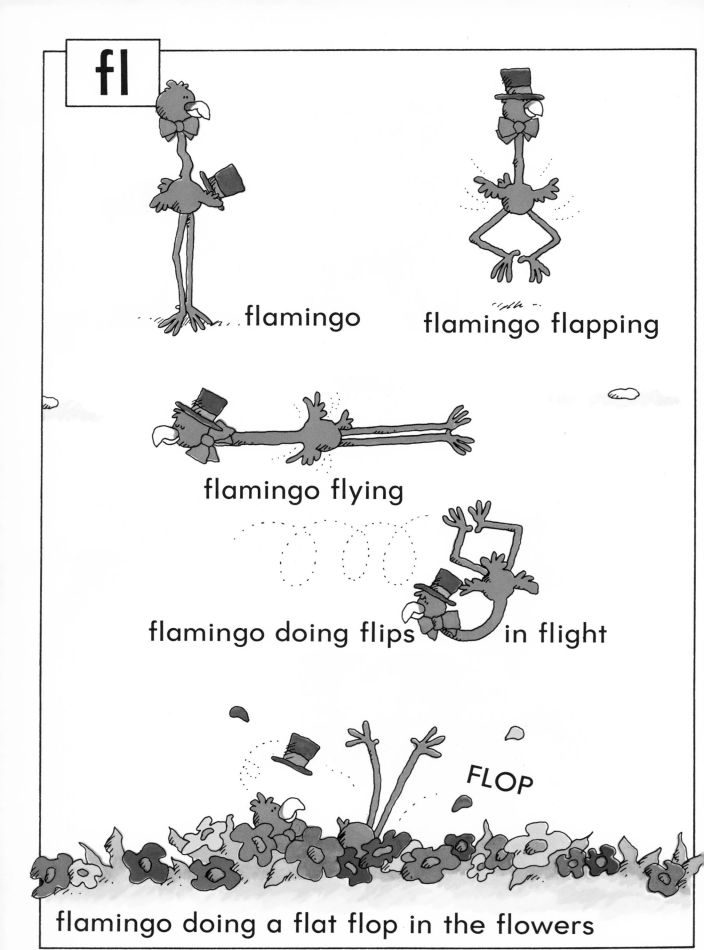

fl

flamingo

flamingo flapping

flamingo flying

flamingo doing flips in flight

FLOP

flamingo doing a flat flop in the flowers

frowning frog

FROM FROG

fresh fruit from frog

frolicking to

frolicking fro

frolicking to and fro

frog friends

groundhogs greeting groundhogs

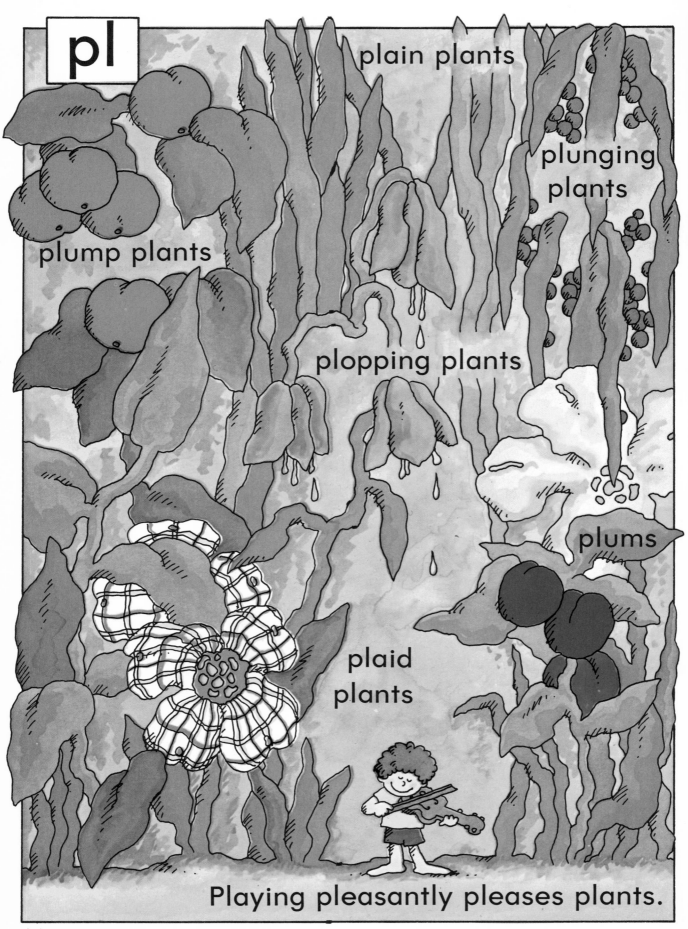

pl

plain plants

plunging
plants

plump plants

plopping plants

plums

plaid
plants

Playing pleasantly pleases plants.

44

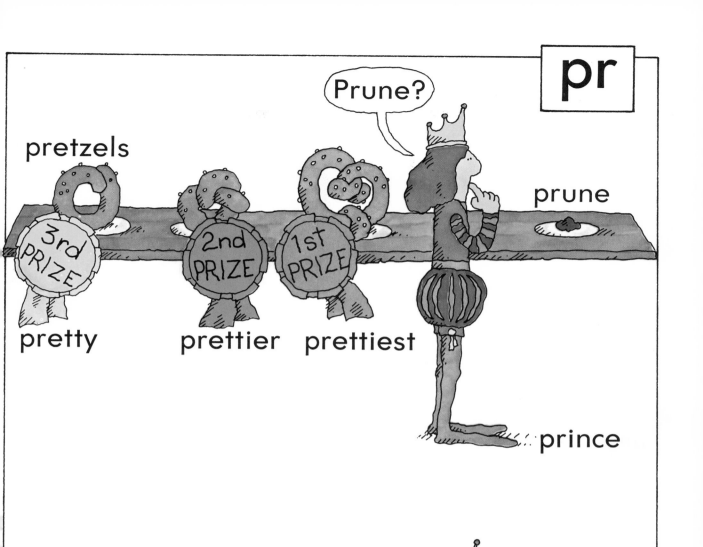

pretzels

Prune?

prune

pretty   prettier   prettiest

prince

The prince presents
the prize pretzel
to the princess.

The princess probably prefers the prune.

dr

The dreaded dragon dreams.

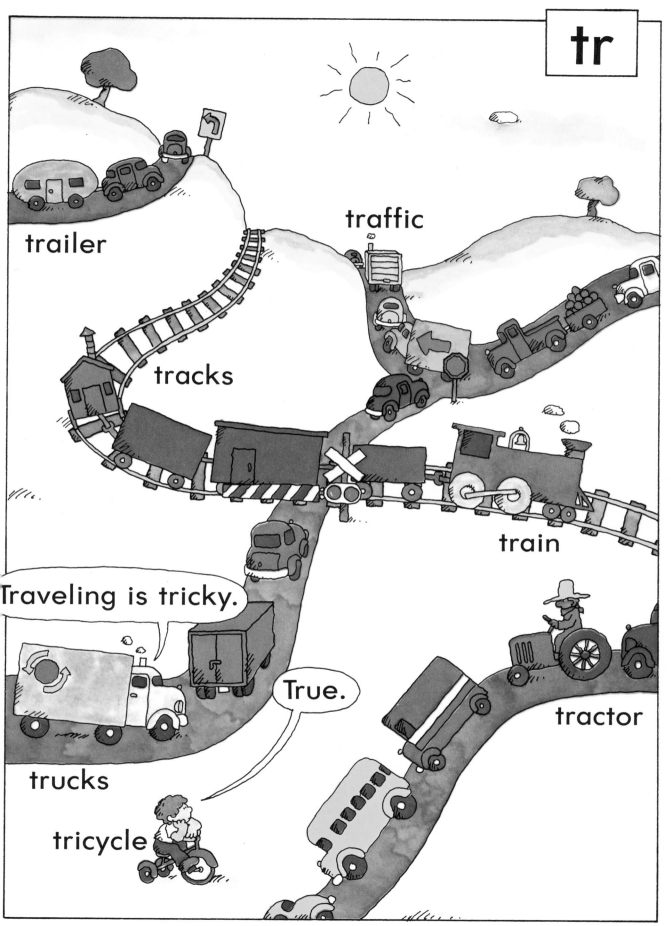

tr

trailer

traffic

tracks

train

Traveling is tricky.

True.

trucks

tricycle

tractor

47

twelve twins tweeting on twig

twelve twins twirling on twig

twelve twins all a-twitter

swans swimming

SWOOSH

swan in a swift swoop

SWOON

swan's sweetheart in a swoon

swan in a swirl

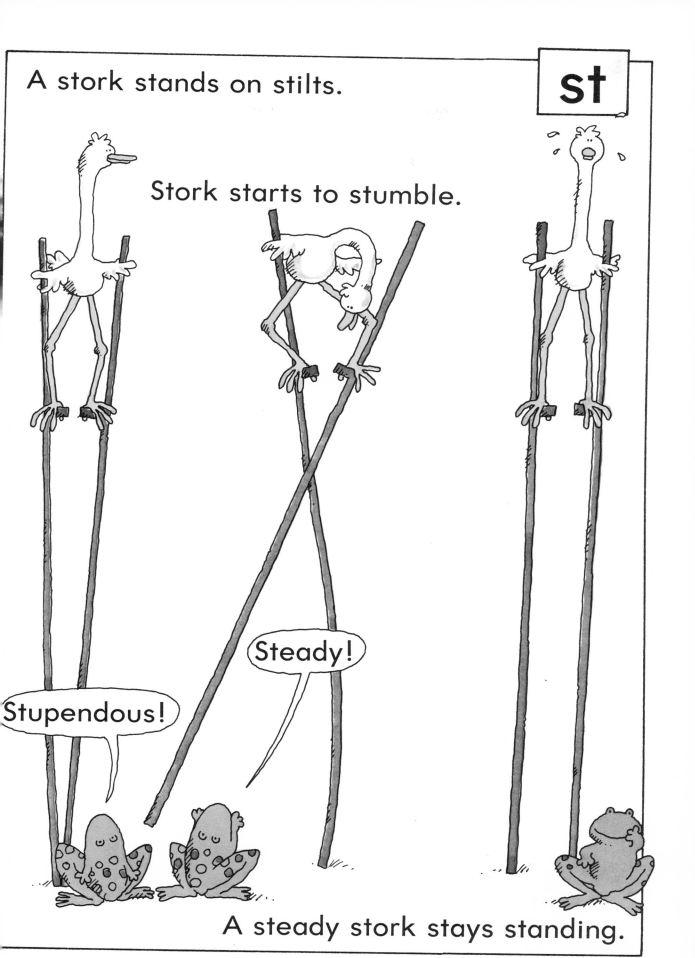

snakes snug in sneakers snatching snoozes

scary scooters

The Scariest Scooter Ever

skating skunk

skiing skunk

skipping skunk

sketching skunk

skin diving skunk

A skunk is skillful.

squirrel

square

squirrel squeezing square

SQUEAK

SQUEAL

The squeaky square gets the squirrel.

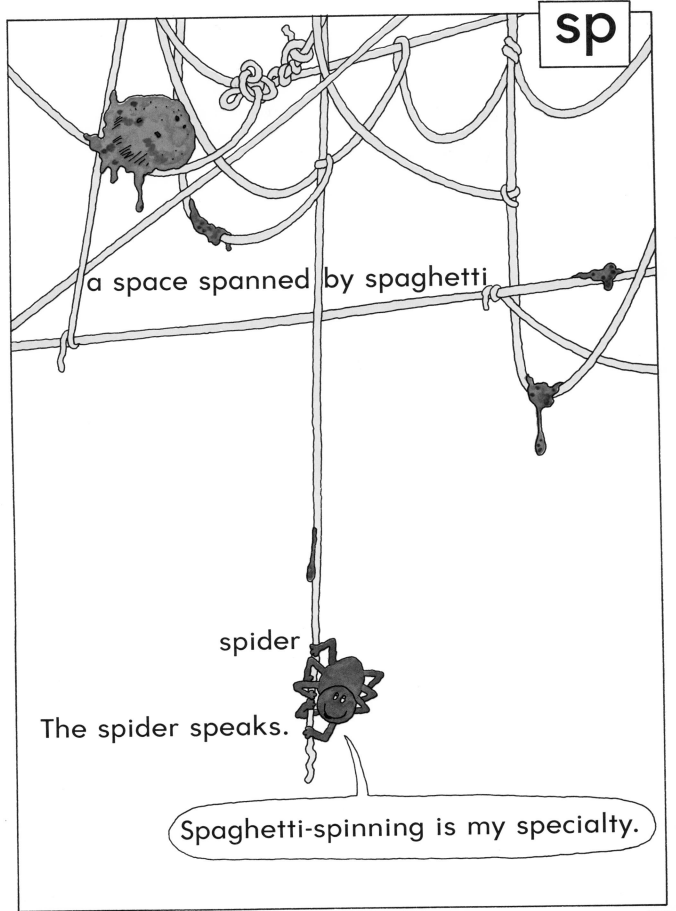

sp

a space spanned by spaghetti

spider

The spider speaks.

Spaghetti-spinning is my specialty.

spl

splits

SPLISH

SPLASH

SPLOSH

Splits make a splendid splash.

sprout

sprinkling sprout

sprout springs up

sprout spreads out

sprout

strong strawberry

strong strawberry struggling with string

strikingly strong strawberry

Strength in strawberries is strange.

SCREECH

SCREECH

scrawny screechers

scraps

a scramble over scraps

screechers with scrapes and scratches

black	flying	scratches	square
blob	fresh	screech	squeak
blowing	friends	skating	squeeze
breakfast	frog	skunk	squirrel
breaks	from	slippery	stands
bringing	fruit	sloppy	starts
broken	glad	small	stays
brownies	glamorous	smart	strange
cleaning	grandma	smash	string
climbing	grandpa	smile	strong
clocks	grouch	smooth	swan
closet	grumble	snakes	swimming
crash	plants	snore	tracks
crumbs	playing	space	tractor
crunch	pleases	spaghetti	train
dragon	pretty	speaks	tricycle
dreams	prince	spider	trucks
flat	princess	splash	true
flips	prize	splits	tweet
flop	scary	spreads	twelve
flowers	scrapes	springs	twins

62

When pictures for sounds were invented,
there were more sounds than pictures.
There still are.

A few consonant sounds
do not have a letter of their own.
To show these special sounds,
we use two letters together for one sound.
The two letters together
stop standing for their own sounds.
There is no **c** sound or **h** sound
in the word **cheese**.
The **ch** stands for a special sound.
Sometimes special sounds
are blended with **r**.

ch

 children

 chocolate chunks

children chewing chocolate chunks

champion
chocolate chunk chewer

sheep showering

sheep shampooing

sheep shining shoes

Show me a showered and shampooed sheep
with shiny shoes,
and I'll show you a sheep in sharp shape.

whiz on wheels

69

thr

Thread thrills
three thrushes
through and through.

shrill
shrieks

shrub

The shrub shrinker shrugs.

The shrub shrinker shrinks.

champion	showering	thief	whack
chewing	shrieks	things	what
children	shrill	think	wheels
chocolate	shrink	this	wheeze
chunk	shrivel	those	when
shampooing	shrub	thought	where
shape	shrugs	thread	whistle
sharp	thanks	three	whiz
sheep	that's	thrills	who
shiny	theirs	through	whole
shoes	there	thrushes	whose
show	these	thump	why

72

There is no **k** sound
in the word **knew**.
Take away the consonant **k**
and the word isn't the same.
Now it's **new**.
Spelling usually follows the code,
but sometimes it's odd.
In the odd spelling **kn**,
only the **n** sound is heard.
In the odd spelling **ph**,
an **f** sound is heard.

Odd spellings may look strange,
but they are used for the same sounds over and over
in many different words.

kn

nine knights

nine knapsacks

nine knobs

nine knocks

Why do knights knock?

Nobody knows.

74

gnats

gnu

gnats on gnu

Gnu nets gnats.

not nice for gnats

Gnu nets gnu too.

not nice for gnu

rh

A rhinoceros with rhythm is rare.

wren

wreath

wriggling into wreath

wrapped up in wreath

wrestling out of wreath

Wrestling really wrecks a wreath.

ghosts

ghastly ghost

ghastlier ghost

ghastliest ghost

gh

ghastly　　knobs　　phone　　　　　wreath

ghost　　　knock　　photographer　wrecks

gnats　　　knots　　rhinoceros　　wren

gnu　　　　knows　　rhythm　　　　wrestling

knights　　phantom　wrapped　　　wriggling

80

Beginning Vowels:
Long Sounds And Short Sounds

There are only five beginning vowels.

a e i o u

Sometimes **y** is a vowel,

but not at the beginning of a word.

Although there are only five

(and sometimes six) vowels,

there are many vowel sounds.

Each vowel has a long sound

which is the same sound you hear

when you say the name of the letter.

a e i o u

Those are the long sounds.

Each vowel has a short sound, too.

Most of the time a vowel stands for

either its long sound

or its short sound.

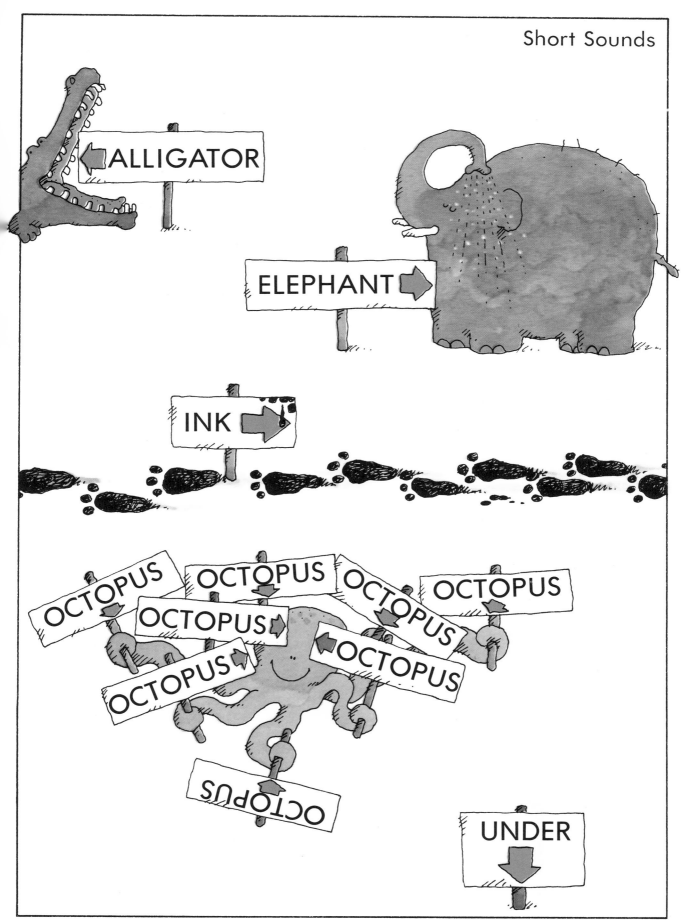

anteater adding apples

angry anteater angry at anaconda

An anteater is absurd.

anteater admiring answer

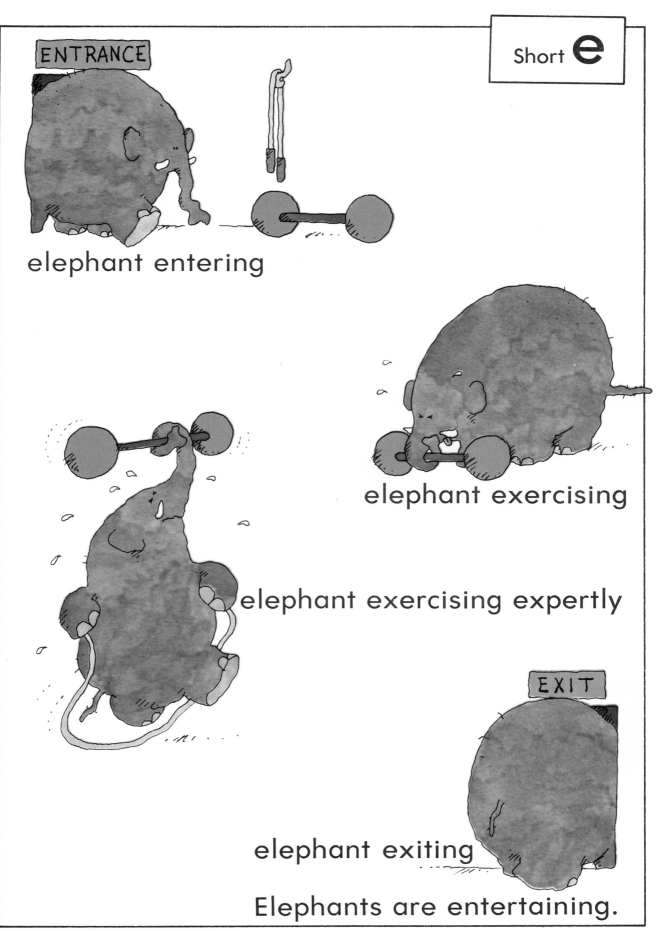

elephant entering

elephant exercising

elephant exercising expertly

elephant exiting

Elephants are entertaining.

87

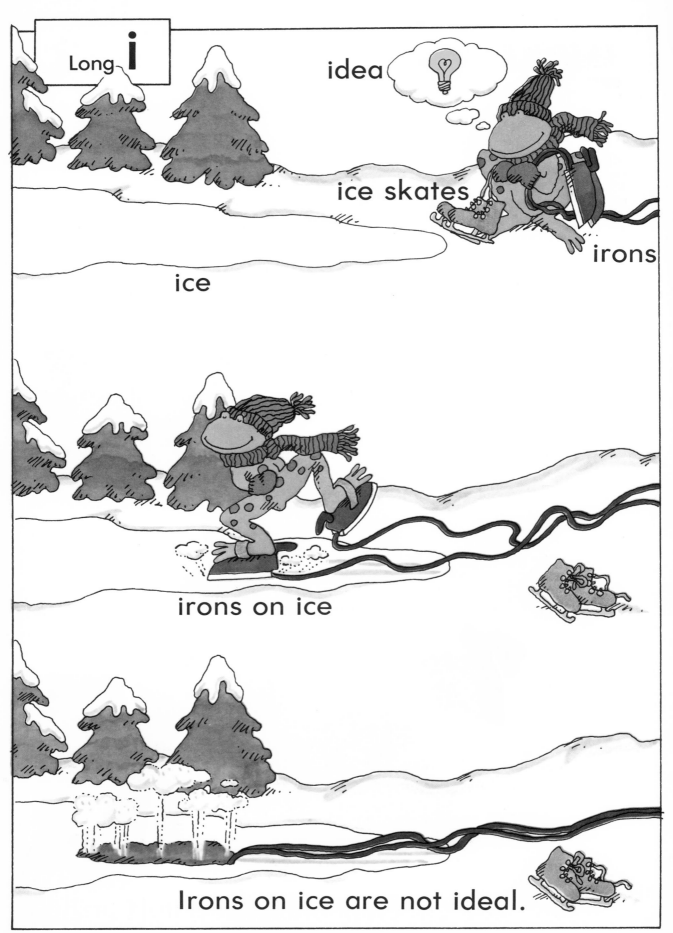

Long **i**

idea

ice skates

irons

ice

irons on ice

Irons on ice are not ideal.

88

octopus
with oxfords on

octopus
with oxfords off

octopus
with oxfords on
and oxfords off

the opposite

Octopuses are odd.

ukulele

using ukelele   on unicycle

useless unicycle   useless ukelele

using useless unicycle on useless ukulele

umbrella

uncle under umbrella

uncle under upside-down umbrella

upside-down uncle under upside-down umbrella
Uncle is unusual.

adding
alligator
an
anaconda
angry
answer
anteater
ape
apples
apron
at
ate
eel
elephant

entering
entertaining
even
evil
exercising
exiting
ice
idea
ideal
ink
inside
interesting
invention
inventor

invisible
irons
is
isn't
it
it's
ivy
ocean
octopus
odd
off
old
on
only

opposite
overcoat
owner
oxfords
ukulele
umbrella
uncle
under
unicorn
unicycle
unusual
upside-down
useless
using